ZORA NEALE HURSTON

Author and Anthropologist

Celebrating **BLACK ARTISTS**

ZORA NEALE HURSTON

Author and Anthropologist

Enslow Publishing
101 W. 23rd Street
Suite 240
New York, NY 10011
USA

enslow.com

CHARLOTTE ETINDE-CROMPTON AND SAMUEL WILLARD CROMPTON

Published in 2020 by Enslow Publishing, LLC.
101 W. 23rd Street, Suite 240, New York, NY 10011

Copyright © 2020 by Enslow Publishing, LLC.

All rights reserved.

No part of this book may be reproduced by any means without the written permission of the publisher.

Library of Congress Cataloging-in-Publication Data

Name: Crompton, Samuel Willard, author. | Etinde-Crompton, Charlotte, author.
Title: Zora Neale Hurston : author and anthropologist / Samuel Willard Crompton and Charlotte Etinde-Crompton.
Description: New York : Enslow Publishing, [2020] | Series: Celebrating Black artists | Audience: Grades 7–12. | Includes bibliographical references and index.
Identifiers: LCCN 2018020369| ISBN 9781978503595 (library bound) | ISBN 9781978505346 (pbk.)
Subjects: LCSH: Hurston, Zora Neale—Juvenile literature. | African American women novelists—Biography—Juvenile literature. | Folklorists—United States—Biography—Juvenile literature. | LCGFT: Biographies.
Classification: LCC PS3515.U789 Z68 2019 | DDC 813/.52 [B] —dc23
LC record available at https://lccn.loc.gov/2018020369

Printed in China

To Our Readers: We have done our best to make sure all website addresses in this book were active and appropriate when we went to press. However, the author and the publisher have no control over and assume no liability for the material available on those websites or on any websites they may link to. Any comments or suggestions can be sent by email to customerservice@enslow.com.

Photo Credits: Cover, pp. 3, 24–25 Corbis Historical/Getty Images; p. 8 Fotosearch/Archive Photos/Getty Images; pp. 10, 18–19, 26–27, 31, 40–41, 65 Library of Congress Prints and Photographs Division Washington, D.C.; p. 14 FloNight (Sydney Poore)/Wikimedia Commons/File: Eatonville,_Florida_Town_Hall_sign_marker/CC BY-SA 4.0; pp. 20–21 Leemage/Corbis Historical/Getty Images; p. 34 Private Collection/Prismatic Pictures/Bridgeman Images; p. 36 ullstein bild/Getty Images; p. 45 Graveyardwalker (Amy Walker)/Wikimedia Commons/File: Bronze_bust_of_Cudjoe_Lewis/CC BY-SA 4.0; p. 50 Library of Congress/Corbis Historical/Getty Images; p. 57 Everett Collection Historical/Alamy Stock Photo; p. 58 Interfoto/Alamy Stock Photo; p. 61 AF Archive/Alamy Stock Photo; pp. 68–69 Jack Vartoogian/Archive Photos/Getty Images; p. 72 The Protected Art Archive/Alamy Stock Photo; p. 75 Smith Collection/Gado/Archive Photos/Getty Images; pp. 78–79 Bettmann/Getty Images; pp. 82–83 Jeff Greenberg/Universal Images Group/Getty Images; p. 86 Anthony Barboza/Archive Photos/Getty Images; pp. 88–89 PhotoQuest/Archive Photos/Getty Images.

Contents

1 Railroad Ties and Long-Haired Ladies 7

2 Triumph and Trauma 13

3 On the Road 22

4 Back in School 30

5 Godmother and Her Children 39

6 Jonah's Vine 49

7 Watching God 56

8 Love and Its Discontents 64

9 Adversity 71

10 Rebirth 81

Chronology 91

Chapter Notes 95

Glossary 98

Further Reading 99

Index 101

About the Authors 104

Chapter 1

Railroad Ties and Long-Haired Ladies

In more than three decades as a top writer, Zora Neale Hurston wrote novels, plays, and countless short stories. At the same time, Hurston was an impressive anthropologist, working on a particularly important project that came to fruition in June 1939. At this time, the Federal Writers' Project (FWP) was hiring numerous writers. Under the umbrella of the Works Progress Administration, the FWP writers collected and reported on specific material for all forty-eight states (Hawaii and Alaska were not yet part of the United States). Hurston was selected to report on Florida.

That Zora Neale Hurston would find employment with the Federal Writers' Project is not surprising. She knew as much about African American life, folklore, and history in Florida as anyone alive. But it is somewhat surprising that she was able to reveal, and highlight, several working-class songs. In June 1939, a

8 ZORA NEALE HURSTON: Author and Anthropologist

In addition to writing fiction, Zora Neale Hurston worked as an anthropologist, studying black American folklore and culture.

set of recordings was made in Jacksonville, Florida, with Hurston's recognizable voice playing the leading role.

The Songs

"Bella Mina" was a song of African American workers who adapted Italian words to the black vernacular. This is followed by "Crow Dance," one of Hurston's favorites. On the recording, she explains that the crow was sacred to various Native American groups, and that they passed this belief on to African Americans they encountered in the Deep South. To enact the performance, Hurston gestured strongly with her arms and uttered some words of the song: "This crow, this crow gonna fly tonight/ See how he flied, fly/ Oh momma come see that crow."[1] The crow was an embodiment of the natural world, but its ability to fly away was a quality envied by many African Americans who wished to do the same.

African American Workers in Florida

The farther into the Deep South one traveled, the more oppressive the conditions became. No one would argue that life in Virginia or Tennessee was positive for African Americans, but Alabama, Georgia, and Mississippi were reckoned just about the worst. Florida was a special case because it had been settled later than its Deep South counterparts. But the sounds of African American songs were far more than of lamentation. There was, as Zora Neale Hurston was quick to point out, an exuberance to African American life that could not be suppressed or denied, despite any number of hardships.

10 ZORA NEALE HURSTON: Author and Anthropologist

Hurston was especially interested in the songs of African American laborers in the South.

Railroad Ties and Long-Haired Ladies

"Crow Dance" was followed by "Dat Old Black Gal," a song among the laborers of the Miami region. It was especially popular with the men of construction crews, driving spikes into railroad ties. The work was performed during intense heat, and it helped the men to build a rhythmic pattern to get them through the afternoon: "Keep on grumbling/ a new pair of shoes, Lord, a new pair of shoes/ I'm gonna give her all my money/ Kisses too."[2]

One can imagine that songs such as this helped the railroad workers get through the day. Another song, "Ever Been Down," didn't require a question mark at the end. For black workers in the Deep South, there was no question that they had struggled and suffered: "Rather be in Tampa/ With the whip-or-will/ Been down so long/ Down don't bother me/ Weep like a willow/ Moan just like a dove."[3]

"Ever Been Down" was followed by "Gonna See My Long-Haired Babe," which entreated workers to "Let those hammers ring, boy."[4] Two men faced each other on the railroad track, with hammers positioned breast to breast. The singing line provides the rhythm. One man is the lead singer. But perhaps the most intriguing of the sixteen recorded songs is "Let the Deal Go Down."

As Hurston explained it, "Let the Deal Go Down" is primarily a game of luck and chance, an apt metaphor for adapting to the rapidly changing, and occasionally arbitrary, circumstances of life. Two principals, called pikers, place bets while the dealer works with his deck of cards: "Put the money on the wood/ And let the deal go down./ When your card get lucky/ Let the deal go down, boy./ I'm going back to 'Bama,/ Let the deal go down, boy."[5] For black citizens who had been given a "bad hand" by institutional racism and systemic oppression, this was an especially potent metaphor.

Recorded on June 18, 1939, these songs—and commentary—are one of the few direct ways one can connect with Zora Neale Hurston. Her talent is known to the millions who have read *Their Eyes Were Watching God* and other books, but her *presence* is often elusive.

Florida Folklore

Hurston had a special opportunity. Born and raised in rural Florida in an all-black township, Hurston knew about African American folklore and was skillful in presenting it to a white audience. One can suggest, however, that there were tension and pain along with success. Being able to move between black and white worlds gave Hurston many opportunities; at the same time, she seldom had a ready-made community: she had to invent one constantly. Hurston was one of many talented African American artists of the first half of the twentieth century. She achieved a high level of success, but it came at a price.

Chapter 2

Triumph and Trauma

Zora Neale Hurston led a complicated life. Right from the beginning, there were discrepancies and variations in the accounts of her life story. One of the few chronological periods where the evidence is straightforward is her earliest years.

Recorded history has suggested that Zora was born in Notasulga, Alabama, on January 7, 1891. But even this was later opened to dispute. Later in life, Zora claimed she was born in Eatonville, Florida, on January 7, 1901, boldly shaving an entire decade off her age. Virtually all the documentary evidence points to 1891, however, and it is extremely likely she was born in rural Alabama, rather than northern Florida.

John Hurston and Lucy Potts married around 1884. Potts was from a land-holding African American family, and Hurston hailed from the wrong side of the "creek" (the expression that meant the same as from the wrong side of the "tracks"). Hurston won over Potts, and they married when she was only sixteen. Displeased with her

14 ZORA NEALE HURSTON: Author and Anthropologist

Eatonville, Florida, where Hurston spent her childhood, was a town populated and governed entirely by black citizens.

daughter's choice, Lucy Potts's mother cut off all contact for a number of years.

Perhaps in 1889, the growing family—there eventually were six boys and two girls—moved from Alabama to Eatonville, Florida. The first incorporated black township in the United States, Eatonville was a rather humble place, about 6 miles (9 kilometers) from Winter Park. But to its African American residents, Eatonville was a stunning example of black success. The town had no white residents, and it was governed by a mayor and town council composed entirely of black citizens.

Triumph and Trauma

Different Approaches

Half a century after it was over, Zora Neale Hurston recalled her childhood in glowing terms. She may have exaggerated some parts and downplayed others, but there is not the slightest doubt that she viewed her childhood as a marvelous time, one that was never equaled in later life:

> There were plenty of orange, grapefruit, tangerine, guavas, and other fruits in our yard. We had a five-acre garden with things to eat growing in it, and so we were never hungry… Our house had eight rooms, and we called it a two-story house, but later on I learned it was really one story and a jump…There were eight children in the family, and our house was noisy from the time school turned out until bedtime.[1]

John Hurston was the star of this big family. A tall, broad-shouldered man who favored Stetson hats, he rose to become first a Baptist minister and then the mayor of Eatonville. In the latter capacity, he helped to write the town laws. John Hurston was the outer show of strength for the family. But its heart and soul belonged to his diminutive wife, five-foot-tall Lucy Potts Hurston:

> Mama exhorted her children at every opportunity to "jump at de sun." We might not land on the sun, but at least we would get off the ground. Papa did not feel so hopeful. Leave well enough alone. It did not do for Negroes to have too much spirit.[2]

This discrepancy is surprising, given all that John Hurston had accomplished. But he was less trusting than his wife, and he seems to have believed that racial segregation—and limited opportunities—would remain the case for the duration of his children's lives.

The difference and discrepancy between her parents' philosophies marked Hurston for life. She would forever follow her mother's admonition, seeking to perform the near impossible, but she never forgot her father's prescription.

The Kindness of Strangers

From an early age, Zora demonstrated high spirit and a desire for adventure. As she remembered it, Zora frequently planted herself at the front door, waiting for passers-by, and when they approached, she greeted them with a friendly hello and a request to go along with them. On most occasions, this Southern friendliness resulted in little more than a polite exchange. Once, however, Zora encountered two white Northern ladies. Seeing and sensing her intellectual hunger, they mailed her all sorts of books, which furnished the beginning of her self-education: "The books gave me more pleasure than the clothes. I had never been too keen on dressing up. It called for hard scrubbings with Octagon soap suds getting in my eyes, and none too gentle fingers scrubbing my neck and gouging in my ears."[3]

While these white women had showed interest in Zora, the African Americans of Eatonville saw Zora as thoroughly one of their own, if a little eccentric.

Triumph and Trauma

As a young woman, Zora was not asked or allowed to spend time on the front porch of Joe Clarke's store, a local hangout, but she spent enough time in the area to gather the rich flavor and dialect of her neighbors. The black men who gathered at the store passed many harmless hours with gossip. Whether it was a budding romance, a family conflict, or a domestic dispute, there always seemed to be much to discuss. Zora may have been frightened by parts of the conversations, but she never said so (either then or in her memoir). The fear she experienced came directly from within:

> I do not know when the visions began. Certainly I was not more than seven years old, but I remember the first coming very distinctly… There was some cool shade on the porch so I sat down, and soon I was asleep in a strange way…I

Local Customs

The Deep South was filled with many superstitious practices around the turn of the twentieth century. This doesn't mean that the Northeast and Midwest were free of such beliefs; rather, there was enough scientific rationalism in those areas to tamp down unusual beliefs. As she became more interested in anthropology and the practices of small Southern black communities, Zora later immersed herself in studying the significance of voodoo.

saw twelve scenes flash before me, each one held until I had seen it in every detail, and then be replaced by another...I knew that they were all true, a preview of things to come, and my soul writhed in agony and shrunk away.[4]

In this dream, vision, or a combination of the two, Zora beheld a future filled with pain. She would love and suffer betrayal. She would be orphaned early and lead a wandering life. She would be friendless and at the mercy of events. But after a great deal of suffering, she would know peace, rest, and understanding.

Because Zora wrote these words many years after the events, one naturally wonders if she unconsciously "edited" their content, adjusting them to fit the times she lived in. But if her vision was legitimate—if she really did experience it at the age of seven—then she was one of those genuine seers whose gifts do not prevent bad things from happening to the "seer."

The Worst Loss

"I knew Mama was sick. She kept getting thinner and thinner, and her chest cold never got any better. Finally, she took to bed."[5] Lucy Potts was worn out, both from the difficulties of eight

Triumph and Trauma

There was a strong sense of fellowship in Eatonville, one that would kindle Hurston's lifelong interest in black communities.

20 ZORA NEALE HURSTON: Author and Anthropologist

Hurston was fascinated by customs and superstitions. She would later go on to study the practice of voodoo in America.

Triumph and Trauma

pregnancies and from the psychological distance from her family of origin. She was only thirty-eight when she died, in the autumn of 1905. Zora Neale Hurston was fourteen years old.

"What years of agony that promise gave me," Zora wrote. "In the first place, I had no idea that it would be soon."[6] In the last hours of her life, Lucy Potts instructed her daughter not to allow the local superstitions to affect her burial. Eatonville residents, like many other rural Florida communities, had a set of special rules, including that mirrors be covered and pillows removed from the bed of a dying person. Zora was unable to fulfill her promise, however. The local women took over in the aftermath of her mother's death. Zora had already experienced a vision of a bleak future. She did not anticipate everything would happen so quickly, however.

Chapter 3

On the Road

No one will ever know the complete story of what Zora Neale Hurston endured between the ages of fourteen and twenty-five. Very likely, those years involved a good deal of suffering that may, at times, have been extreme.

In the immediate aftermath of her mother's death, Zora was sent to Jacksonville, Florida, 130 miles (209 km) from Eatonville. She went to a private school for a while, but her tuition was not paid in time. When Zora looked for a culprit for her predicament, she focused on her stepmother.

A Family Divided

John Hurston was never quite the same after the death of his first wife. But he quickly found a new bride, and she was twenty-three. Local gossips suggested that John Hurston found this young woman all too easily and quickly—that he must have had a previous affair. No one has ever been able to discern the truth of this matter, but it should be said that Reverend Hurston was a "man's man," quite susceptible to the temptations posed to a man of the cloth.

Returning home, Zora got into her first brawl with her stepmother. This one was largely verbal, but a few years later it was followed by a knockdown, drag-out fight that Zora won decisively (she had long been known for her strong arms and fists). Years later, Zora described her teen years, remarking on her physical strength:

> I discovered that I was extra strong by playing with girls near my age. I had no way of judging the force of my playful blows, and so I was always hurting somebody. Then they would say I meant to hurt, and go home and leave me. Everything was all right, however, when I played with boys. It was a shameful thing to admit being hurt among them. I was the one girl who could take a good pummeling without running home to tell.[1]

The "victory" she won in that last fight was bittersweet at best: Zora was immediately exiled from her family home.

Zora was sad to leave. She was equally sad to witness her father's decline. Physically, John Hurston still looked the part of Baptist minister and town leader, but he was weak on the inside. Whether he was happy in his second marriage remains uncertain, but it seems likely that he pined for his first wife, the one who had kept him on the straight and narrow.

24   ZORA NEALE HURSTON: Author and Anthropologist

On the Road 25

Hurston briefly lived in Jacksonville, Florida.

Hurston lived with her brother Bob and his family in Memphis, Tennessee, for a short while.

On the Road   27

Escape After Escape

In one regard, John and Lucy Hurston had succeeded beyond their own expectations. The Hurston children—all eight of them—did "jump at de sun." They took for granted that many good, even wonderful, things were possible. Though her elder sister, Sarah, was also exiled from the family home, Zora Neale Hurston's brothers were rising in the world.

Hurston went to live with one brother in Jacksonville, Florida, for a short time. She then traveled to Memphis, Tennessee, to live at the home of her eldest brother, Bob, his wife, and their first child. Bob Hurston promised to send his younger sister to school, but this pledge quickly faded. Zora Neale Hurston found herself acting as a babysitter and house cleaner for her brother and sister-in-law.

The earliest photograph of Hurston to survive dates from this time. She stands on the left, with her brother on the right and her sister-in-law and child in between. One does not wish to read too much into a photograph, but Hurston seems depressed. This is one of the few photographs—from her entire lifetime—when she looks *older* than her actual years. Exactly how she "escaped" her elder brother is unknown, but this episode did not fracture their relationship, as they stayed in touch. Then, at about the age of twenty, Zora Neale Hurston simply disappeared.

The Missing Years

During this period, Hurston seemed to vanish from the physical and geographic map. She was not listed in the US Census. Nor was there any public record of her whereabouts. She vanished completely from history. In her autobiography, Hurston wrote cryptically about a "shotgun house" and a time of great misery (memories of the former appear to surface in Hurston's play *Poker!*). The chances are that this particular period of difficulty transpired during her missing years.

Had Hurston entered into some type of informal marriage or living arrangement with a man? And if so, was she abused by this unnamed and unknown man in her life? Opinion on this matter is split down the middle. Hurston did suffer from low self-esteem during this part of her life; it is revealed in the earliest photograph to survive, which shows her with her brother and sister-in-law. But Hurston was also a very physical person. She had been known as something of a bully in her Eatonville years, more than ready to take up fists, even with the neighborhood boys. That she could become a caged person, subjected to the whims of a powerful man, seems unlikely. What does seem likely, however, is that the missing years were a time of deep pain and that Hurston carried a burden of shame for the rest of her life. Though she would write hundreds of letters and inspire numerous conversations, she never once described these years. In fact, she sought to erase them completely.

Chapter 4

Back in School

Throughout her life, Zora Neale Hurston held a divided opinion where school was concerned. As a young person, she thirsted for knowledge; as a middle-aged woman, she lamented the emphasis on certifications and degrees. But when she gained an opportunity to study in her late twenties, she seized it with both hands.

Informal Education

At about the age of twenty-five, Hurston got a temporary job with a traveling theater group. Performing both Shakespeare plays and vaudeville skits, the group—whose name has slipped through the cracks of historical memory—was an eye-opener for Hurston. For the first time, she was surrounded by people who cared deeply about learning of all kinds.

Working as a makeup artist, Hurston learned about the finer points of theater. As an informal counselor

Back in School 31

After transferring to Howard University, Hurston became part of a discussion group on African American cultural matters.

for various actors, she came to realize that even more fortunate people had their problems. And the many days spent on the tour bus were much more fun than her previous travels.

After a year and a half on the road, Hurston was discharged from the acting group. This was no fault of her own; rather, the lead actress, who had become her sponsor, gave up the traveling life. Suddenly, at about twenty-eight years old, Hurston was stranded, with nowhere to go. But she recognized the opportunity she had received:

> The experience had matured me in other ways. I had seen, I had been privileged to see folks substitute love for failure of career. I would listen to one and another pour out their feelings sitting on a stool backstage between acts and scenes. Then too, I had seen careers filling up the empty holes left by love…Those experiences, though vicarious, made me see things and think.[1]

Zora Neale Hurston was a true professional when it came to making do with her lot in life. She found work as a manicurist in Washington, D.C., and then migrated to Baltimore, where she entered Morgan Academy in 1917. Though the academy later became part of Morgan State University, it was intended for teenagers. Hurston concealed her age, shaving roughly ten years off so that she could attend.

Many scholars have wondered: How did Zora pull it off? How did she manage to lop ten years off her age and persuade people of it? Zora had plenty of physical vitality, so she may have looked a decade younger than her true age. What may have helped were her infectious laughter and enthusiasm. It is possible that some of her contemporaries were *not* fooled; however, they chose to overlook this mostly harmless deception.

Formal Studies

Once enrolled, Hurston was an enthusiastic student. She felt at a disadvantage where clothes and social status were concerned, but she made up for it with a keen and flexible mind. Her teachers recognized her talent but lamented her tendency to squeak by with less than she was capable of (a charge that would be repeated by others, including work supervisors).

Transferring from Morgan Academy to Howard University, Hurston continued her rapid uphill movement. She did well in her formal studies, and she became part of a discussion group on African American cultural matters, chaired by the formidable Alain Locke, the first African American to win a Rhodes Scholarship. Hurston did not open her heart to many of her new acquaintances; however, the pain and trauma of earlier years had left its mark.

What she lacked in openness, Hurston more than made up for in literary talent. This became evident with the publication of her short story "Spunk," which won second prize in a competition in *Opportunity* magazine in 1925. "Spunk" comes straight from Hurston's childhood in Eatonville, Florida. Many times, she had commented on the importance of Joe Clark's store, the place where the local men gathered to swap stories, boasts, and gossip. In "Spunk," Hurston brings to life a rambunctious and assertive young black man who works at a local sawmill:

> That's one thing Ah likes about Spunk Banks—he ain't skeered of nothin' on God's green footstool—nothin'! He rides that log down at

34 ZORA NEALE HURSTON: Author and Anthropologist

It was during her time at Howard University that Hurston met scholar and writer Alain Locke.

saw-mill jus' like he struts 'round wid another man's wife—jus' don't give a kitty.[2]

Hurston's ear for language is immediately affecting. The language jumps right out at the reader. She does not attempt to formalize African American dialect—rather, she celebrates it. In this, she was among the first. The story is poignant and short. Spunk runs off with another man's wife, and when the wronged husband comes for vengeance, he is quickly killed. But Spunk does not get away with his crime. The sawmill machine he handles so well turns on him, and he is also killed. "Spunk" brought Hurston all the way from Washington, D.C., to New York City.

Meeting a Mentor

Precisely how Zora Neale Hurston "landed" in New York City remains rather mysterious. She later claimed she arrived with only a dollar or two in her pocket. But she came to Manhattan early in 1925, the year consistently associated with the launch of the Harlem Renaissance.

Hurston had earned an associate's degree from Howard University by the time she enrolled at Barnard College, the prestigious sister school of Columbia University. Again, she was self-conscious about her lack of money and clothing when compared with the other students. But Barnard exposed Hurston to one of the most important mentors of her life, Franz Boas.

Born in Germany, Franz Boas came to the United States as a young man. After a sparkling career as a student, he embarked on the work of a lifetime: the

Franz Boas was a mentor to Zora Neale Hurston as she continued her studies in anthropology at Columbia University.

> ## Overcoming Reluctance
>
> It's probably not shocking to most readers that, in Zora Neale Hurston's time, many white Americans thought black stories and legends were unimportant. But while African Americans of the era might have recognized the personal significance of their culture and folklore, they were often reticent about sharing these stories with outsiders. Hurston eventually succeeded to a great degree, but in her early years of collecting folklore, she encountered resistance from the very people who had the most to offer. Only later did she realize that she had been too academic and formal in her approach, when what she really needed was to immerse herself in the culture and its lore to be able transmit it to others.

marriage of archaeology, history, and anthropology. Blessed with a tremendous work ethic, "Papa" Boas required the same from all his serious students. He and Hurston did not always see eye to eye, but they were well-matched enough to inspire one another.

One of Hurston's first field experiments was conducted in Harlem. Standing on various street corners, she asked passers-by if she could measure their heads to get a sense of their cranial structures. Solicitation of this kind came naturally to Hurston, who had spent some of her earliest years asking travelers if she could tag along with them.

Professor Boas was charmed by Hurston, but he was also impatient with her. Hurston's talents were so obvious, he declared, that she had to make more of them. For her part, Hurston was content to get A's in the subjects she liked and C's in those she didn't care about. As graduation approached, Boas told Hurston that he had found a fellowship for her. This money would take her to the Deep South, where she could collect and study African American folklore. She did not express elation. Instead, she calmly accepted the opportunity, as if it were a typical everyday occurrence. But it was not. Very few African Americans had ever been paid a dime to examine the folklore of their own people, and almost no women had that experience. Zora Neale Hurston was about to become a true pioneer.

Chapter 5

Godmother and Her Children

Years later, Zora Neale Hurston recalled her first, fumbling attempts to collect African American folklore. "Research is formalized curiosity," Hurston wrote. "It is poking and prying with a purpose. It is a seeking that he who wished may know the cosmic secrets of the world and they that dwell therein."[1]

Many objective anthropologists and archaeologists of that time disagreed. To them, the new academic disciplines were examples of scientific exactitude. But Hurston never intended to become one of these academic types. To her, folklore research meant entering into the lives of the people she studied. She found them in her native Florida.

Polk County

Hurston went back to Eatonville the long way, stopping for a time in Memphis, Tennessee. There, she reconciled

40 ZORA NEALE HURSTON: Author and Anthropologist

Godmother and Her Children

Hurston returned to Florida to begin her field research on black folklore in America.

with her brother Bob, with whom she had parted a decade earlier. He filled her in on the painful aspects of their father's death—he was killed in an automobile accident in Memphis some years earlier. For her part, Hurston brought Bob the news of two of their siblings, who lived in the greater New York area. At the end of the visit, Hurston felt reunited with at least part of her family. The wounds of separation were not entirely healed, but she had made progress.

Proceeding to Eatonville and then to central Florida, Hurston spent a good deal of time in Polk County, just east of Tampa. Years later, she admitted that her initial foray into folkore research was not very successful:

> I did not have the right approach. The glamor of Barnard College was still upon me. I dwelt in marble halls. I knew where the material was all right. But I went about asking, in carefully accented Barnardese, "Pardon me, but do you know any folk-tales or folk-songs?"[2]

The people Zora approached were full of stories and anecdotes. But they did not respond to her until she came out of her college-educated, ivory-tower self to truly engage with them, treating them as equals instead of merely subjects of her research. It soon became clear to Zora that the only way to reach these black men and women—many of whom did not have the benefit of her education and her ascension to the professional, academic class—and gain their trust and document their rich history, was to sit *among* them. The first six months of field research was not as successful as she had hoped.

Hurston recalled that she hung her head and wept when she reported to "Papa" Boas at Barnard. But she was learning the art and craft of folklore collection.

Godmother Mason

Sometime in 1927, Hurston met another larger-than-life mentor: Charlotte Osgood Mason. The results of this relationship were powerful and long lasting.

Heiress to a large fortune, Charlotte Osgood Mason was a formidable, determined, and willful person who wanted to make a difference in the world. Her physician husband, who died twenty years earlier, had given her a profound belief in psychic powers, including telepathy. Thanks to her idyllic childhood and the pain she had suffered since its end, Hurston, too, was a believer in extrasensory powers:

> Laugh if you will, but there was and is a psychic bond between us. She could read my mind, not only when I was in her presence, but thousands of miles away...The thing that delighted her was the fact that I was her only Godchild who could read her thoughts at a distance...She was just as pagan as I.[3]

In a matter of weeks after their first meeting, Hurston was on Godmother Mason's payroll. Godmother—an affectionate title she forced all of her charges to call her—gave Hurston $150 per month on the understanding that Hurston not publish any material without specific permission. In spite of this red flag—one that would augur many conflicts to come in the future—Hurston accepted the offer.

Godmother Mason had previously been enamored of Native American life and culture, but by the 1920s, she was most interested in all things African. Most particularly, Godmother wanted to establish a "bridge to Africa," one that would bring all the energy and vitality of the African tribespeople to twentieth-century America. Both she and her late husband felt that Western rationalism had killed white imagination and spirituality. Though her financial patronage of African Americans was seen as a politically progressive and philanthropic move at the time, Godmother Mason's belief rested on an uncomfortable fetishization of the "primitive" creativity of black artists. Nevertheless, Mason's money allowed

Belief in Primitivism

Godmother Mason was an extreme case of a general phenomenon. In the 1920s, many Americans believed that twentieth-century life had become too technological and complex. Many argued that a return to "primitive" methods, beliefs, and attitudes was necessary. For Charlotte Osgood Mason, this meant supporting black artists in the hopes of reinvigorating American culture choked by white society's focus on reason and rationality.

Godmother and Her Children 45

In the late 1920s, Hurston met with former slave Cudjo Lewis and interviewed him at length, using that material for what would become *Barracoon: The Story of the Last "Black Cargo"* (2018).

Hurston to return to Florida, and to do so largely on her own terms.

A Concealed Deception

On her previous trip to the South, in 1926, Hurston had met a remarkable person: an elderly African American man named Cudjo Lewis (also known as Kossula, his African name) who was widely believed to be the last survivor of the last slave ship to arrive in the Southern states prior to the Civil War. Hurston used this material for an article in the *Journal of Negro History*. This interview should have been the high point and highlight of that research trip. But it was not. Hurston plagiarized much of this research material from Emma Langdon Roche's *Historic Sketches of the Old South*—and the stories Hurston had recounted therein were not even about Lewis.

Precisely why Hurston did this remains unclear. Some scholars go as far as suggesting that she wanted to be caught, that she felt unworthy of her recent success. More likely, however, is that she lost her original notes, and found it necessary to examine and use other scholars' material to supplement her own. Was she in the wrong? Beyond the shadow of a doubt.

Plagiarism is one of the most serious charges that can be leveled at a scholar. To be regarded as a serious researcher, one must use original materials in an original way, not copy from someone else. Of course, there are times when one writer's phrases are like another's. But direct copying is strictly forbidden. This makes it all the more remarkable that Hurston got away with it. Her plagiarism was not discovered in her lifetime.

Sophomore Success

By her second research trip in 1928, Hurston had become much more adept at connecting with local communities—and more careful about producing original work. She realized that one could not pry, or wrestle, experience out of rural African Americans. Rather, she needed to enter their experience and learn from it.

With Godmother Mason's generous allowance, Hurston revisited Cudjo Lewis, interviewing him extensively, faithfully documenting their conversations, and filming Lewis on a 16-millimeter camera. (This latter work became a brief silent film, entitled *Kossula: Last of the Takoi Slaves*—though Hurston was unhappy with its quality and thus never showed it publicly or wrote of its existence.) Based on their discussions, Hurston published a short article about Lewis's life, "The Last Slave Ship," in the *American Mercury*. But she was far from done with Cudjo Lewis. Hurston would go on to use this material in a full-length biography of Lewis called *Barracoon: The Story of the Last "Black Cargo."* For years, Hurston attempted to find a home for this work. It was finally published by HarperCollins in May 2018, nearly fifty years after Hurston's death.

On this productive second trip south, numerous successes followed. Hurston became acquainted with many black Americans with interesting and profound stories to relate. One of the most fascinating, which has not survived in documentary form, is the story of a black man who fashioned his entire Florida home in the shape of a living sculpture. Faced with such fascinating men and women, Hurston's enthusiasm grew. But that enthusiasm was all too rapidly brought to heel by Godmother Mason.

Chapter 6

Jonah's Vine

Godmother Charlotte Mason was very careful with how she spent her money. She was pleased to support African American artists such as Zora Neale Hurston, Langston Hughes, and Alain Locke—just as long as they toed the line and obeyed her instructions. This meant keeping accurate accounts of what they spent and submitting them to Godmother at regular intervals. Unfortunately, while she possessed many talents, Zora Neale Hurston was a poor record-keeper.

Serious Conflicts

Hurston already had a major conflict with the poet Langston Hughes, formerly her good friend. At certain times, they delighted in each other's company. But in 1930, a disagreement arose over literary ownership of *Mule Bone*, a play they had written together. Even today, with nearly a century for examination, it is difficult to say who was right and who was wrong. One thing can

Though Zora Neale Hurston considered poet Langston Hughes to be a friend, the two had a falling out over the ownership of their cowritten play, *Mule Bone*.

be said with confidence, however: Hurston was casual with ownership to literary properties, just as she was with financial accounts.

Mule Bone eventually was accepted as Hurston's intellectual property, but the wrangling led to a permanent estrangement from Langston Hughes. Hurston and Hughes both lamented the loss of their friendship. Occasionally, they attempted to patch things up, but all their efforts were in vain.

Godmother Mason, too, had accounts to settle: She broke with Langston Hughes in 1930, and she put Hurston on probation that same year. But unlike Hughes, Hurston never made a complete break with Godmother Mason. In letter after letter, she used flattery and compliments, appealing to Mason's pride. But Hurston, too, eventually felt the full force of Charlotte Osgood Mason's wrath. She was cut off from financial assistance in 1932.

The stock market crash happened in the autumn of 1929, but it was not until 1930 that its full effects were felt. For Hurston, who was long accustomed to getting by on the friendship and help of strangers, the advent of the Depression was a severe blow. It should be noted, however, that her writing—which had done quite well in the late 1920s—took a major step forward in the 1930s, even without the patronage of her capricious godmother.

Jonah's Gourd Vine

Having experienced success with short stories, Zora Neale Hurston turned her attention to writing a novel.

In 1934, Philadelphia publisher J. B. Lippincott brought out *Jonah's Gourd Vine*, her first full-length book.

"God was grumbling his thunder and playing the zig-zag lightning thru his fingers."[1] The opening words of the novel suggest its engaging and impressive style. Hurston knew how to employ a phrase, and she was adept at incorporating more than one thought into a single sentence. "God was grumbling his thunder" sounds as "proper" as a writer wishing to be part of the (inarguably largely white) literary tradition could be, but "the zig-zag lighting thru his fingers" shows Hurston's skillful use of African American expressions. The spelling of "thru" is no accident. From the first sentence, Hurston wishes the reader to know this is not an ordinary novel.

Gourd Vine clearly has significant autobiographical traces. The protagonist, John Pearson, is an African American man a good deal like Hurston's father, John Hurston. Lucy Potts is a lot like her mother, of the same name. But if the novel were strictly autobiographical, it would never have succeeded. Publishers, as well as book reviewers, were very skeptical about memoirs of any sort and tended only to accept those written by the truly rich and famous. J. B. Lippincott & Co. took a chance on Hurston because her narrative and linguistic skill shone forth. The interplay of "proper" English and African American idiom is shown at the beginning of the ninth chapter:

> "You Lucy!" Emmeline scolded as she struggled along behind John and Lucy on the way from church. "Ain't Ah done tole yuh and tole yuh nt

tuh let no boys be puttin' dey hand all very uh? You John! Yu stay arm-length from dat gal and talk it out. You got uh tongue."

Lucy and John sniggered together slyly and walked an inch or two farther apart.

"Good Gawd, dey could drive uh double team between us now," John complained.

"Talk loud. Ah don't 'low no wispering' tuh no gal uh mine."[2]

With the distance established by roughly a century, the modern reader is not surprised to see the use of African American dialect. But in 1934, this was little short of revolutionary. Publishers, critics, and public speakers all accented the importance of formal American English. Almost no magazine, book, or set of articles openly declared the African American vernacular as a valid form of expression, yet Hurston managed to make it work without needing (or wanting) to tidy it up for a white literary readership.

Hurston was so skillful a writer that she did not need long sections of description in order to make her novel work. Instead, she plunged the reader straight into the world she knew so well—that of African Americans in Florida, people struggling to get by who maintained plenty of (quiet) pride. White people do not appear very often in *Gourd Vine*; the scene, setting, and conversation primarily echo the life experiences of Southern blacks. This was thoroughly a tale of black America.

Hurston was also highly versatile in shifting from black American dialect to the more formalized academic language she acquired as a scholar at Barnard (in modern parlance, this is often referred to as "code switching"). But one senses more than just a stylistic shift in her authorial voice when she asserts:

> Whereas in Egypt the coming of the locust made desolation, in the farming South the departure of the Negro laid waste the agricultural industry, crops rotted, houses careened crazily in their utter desertion, and grass grew up in streets. On to the North! The Land of promise.[3]

It seems clear that Hurston was not sorry for the change that took place. She herself was part of the

A Daughter of Florida

Hurston is generally acknowledged as the master of her art: the telling of African American stories from the 1920s and 1930s. While she could have taken on the entire South with her keen mind and attention to detail, from her letters to friends one gathers that Florida was the jewel in her crown—the apple of her literary eye. Certainly, there are aspects of her writing that could transfer well to other states of the Deep South, but her special gift lay in the conversational style of Florida's black community.

Great Migration, which brought so many black men and women from the rural South to the Northern cities.

Startling Success

J. B. Lippincott, Hurston's publisher, had modest hopes for *Jonah's Gourd Vine*. But the reviews that crossed the editor's desk, and the many copies that were sold, persuaded Lippincott that Zora Neale Hurston was a publishing phenomenon, an African American writer whose voice could move from the black community to an even wider one.

"Jonah's Gourd Vine… is an enjoyable novel," a prominent African American newspaper declared. "If you are trying to keep up with Aframerican fiction, you cannot afford to miss it. If you read for amusement, you will cheat yourself out of some sweet hours in your favorite armchair should you let the book get away from you."

The review was quite positive, but its writer took an occasional swipe at Hurston's narrative style. The protagonist, John Pearson, never clearly emerges, the review declares, and the book is more enjoyable than complete.

Though she was less than thrilled, Hurston was careful not to respond to this criticism. Like most black writers, she knew that one of the keys to success was, unfortunately, keeping one's mouth closed—at least some of the time.

Chapter 7

Watching God

In the early 1930s, having won a fellowship from the Julius Rosenwald Fund, Hurston was able to cut most—but not all—of ties to Godmother Mason. In most of their correspondence, Hurston was excessively flattering, referring to her patron as "Darling Godmother." Only in the occasional letter to friends did she reveal the truth, that she felt tethered by the "tigress of Park Avenue."[1]

Inspiration in the Caribbean

Thanks to the Rosenwald fellowship, Hurston was able to travel to the Caribbean. Earlier months of research in New Orleans persuaded her that the Caribbean was overlooked as a source of African American folklore and lifeways. She went first to Jamaica, then still part of the British Empire.

Generally speaking, Hurston was disappointed with Jamaica. Though the Maroons—a highly independent people who dwelled in the mountains—fascinated her

Watching God

Hurston was happiest when conducting research in the field.

from a distance, she did not get close enough to observe their customs. She found mainstream Jamaican culture to be a hodgepodge of Anglo and African influences, with the white people and the male side always dominant. Weary of Jamaica, Zora packed her bags and traveled to Haiti, where things were quite different.

Haiti was then—as it is today—one of the poorest places in the Western Hemisphere. But Hurston delighted

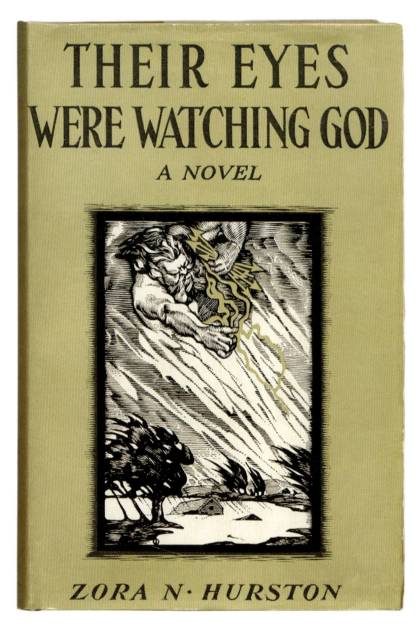

Now considered a classic work of literature, *Their Eyes Were Watching God* was completed in just seven weeks.

in the mixture of cultures—French, Anglo, African, and Creole—and she was predisposed to favor the area because of her anthropological interest in voodoo. This does not necessarily come as a surprise, but what is truly amazing is how deeply inspired Hurston was—and the speed with which she worked. Hurston wrote *Their Eyes Were Watching God* in an intense burst of literary energy in seven short weeks while living in Haiti.

A Complex Heroine

Watching God begins in classic Hurston style, on the front porch of Joe Clarke's store in Eatonville. Just as certain playwrights favor a set-style opening, so did Hurston employ that front porch time and again.

"The men noticed her firm buttocks like she had grape fruits in her hip pockets; the great rope of black hair swinging to her waist and unraveling in the wind like a plume; then her pugnacious breasts trying to bore holes in her shirt."[2] The writing is so evocative and vivid that one does not need a long patch of it—this paragraph opener introduces the reader to Eatonville society at the time of Zora's youth. Excitement, enthusiasm, and joy practically leap off the page. But there is also tragedy at work.

Janie Crawford still looks young, and still impresses men as she walks past the country store, but she is a full-grown woman who has witnessed more than her share of trouble. The men at Clarke's store remember her as the teenage girl who married three times and has now returned to show off her charms. Hurston quickly brings

> ## The Country Store
>
> In early twentieth-century rural Florida, the country store was the setting for more than gossip and titillation. Whether the community was black, such as Eatonville, white, or a more diverse mixture of races and ethnicities, the store served as the meeting place for the local men. Women came to the store, of course, but they did not linger. The country store was where men traded whiskey for molasses, paid their debts to the owner, and swapped stories of rural life. Other parts of the United States had country stores aplenty, but in the Deep South—where no department stores had yet been established—the country store was *the* place, the center of action in the town.

Janie to the woman in whom she confides. The reader gets to experience the previous twenty-five years through the narration of Janie to her friend Phoeby Watson.

This leads the audience to a crucial question: What does God—or a human's observance of God—have to do with all this sensuality? That is precisely what Zora Neale Hurston wanted readers to ask.

Janie's Tortured Past

Janie is a typical black girl in a black township. Her grandmother earnestly wanted her to find the right kind of man and avoid the terrible pains and labors that she endured. But as they often do, the best-laid plans go astray.

Some of the most affecting, and powerful, words come early in the novel. In the second chapter, Hurston describes Janie Crawford's sixteen-year-old vision of love and marriage:

> She was stretched on her back beneath the pear tree soaking in the alto chant of the visiting bees, the gold of the sun and the panting breath of the breeze when the inaudible voice of it all came to her. She saw a dust-bearing bee sink

In 2005, *Their Eyes Were Watching God* was adapted into a film starring Halle Berry.

into the sanctum of a bloom; the thousand sister calyxes arch to meet the love embrace and the ecstatic shiver of the tree from root to tiniest branch creaming in every blossom and frothing with delight. So this was a marriage! She had been summoned to behold a revelation.[3]

Janie clearly represents parts of Hurston herself, with her observant and curious nature, but not the whole. Autobiography is at work, but it is so deftly handled that the reader can enter the experience and make it their own. This vision, or daydream, is not the stuff of what Hurston had seen at the age of sixteen. But Janie Crawford will experience plenty of pain.

Janie Crawford has three marriages, all of them unsatisfying to some degree. Her first husband is a dutiful man and attentive to work, but who pays his wife no attention. She doesn't need, or deserve, his attention, his attitude declares. Following his premature death, Janie marries again and this time joins forces with the toughest, most resolute African American fellow in town. He aspires to become the mayor and succeeds. He earns plenty of money but does not enjoy it to the smallest degree. And he will not let his wife enjoy life, either. Janie is regarded as little more than an ornament, a testament to her husband's success.

In her third and final marriage, Janie finds partial happiness. Her third husband, named Tea Cake, is much younger than herself. He knows how to enjoy life, and he shows his wife how to do the same. But tragedy follows Janie even here.

How, the reader wonders, can so much bad luck come to one person? Hurston never answers this question entirely, but the reader senses her belief that experience is more important than success:

> The kiss of his memory made pictures of love and light against the wall. Here was peace. She pulled in her horizon life a great fish-net. Pulled it from around the waist of the world and draped it over her shoulder. So much of life in its meshes! She called in her soul to come and see.[4]

In part, it seems that all of the trials and tragedies that Janie endures, all the ways in which her plans go sideways, serve to underscore her own lack of control—suggesting there is a higher power and a greater plan at work. Here, finally, the reader starts to understand Hurston's point in titling the novel. Published in 1937, *Their Eyes Were Watching God* drew no small measure of negative criticism from other African American writers, like Richard Wright and Ralph Ellison, both of whom believed Hurston failed to take the totality of black life seriously, using her characters merely as props for tragedy and sensuality. It wasn't until the 1970s, when writers like Alice Walker began to take Hurston seriously, that *Their Eyes Were Watching God* became appreciated for the full measure of its artistry.

Chapter 8

Love and Its Discontents

Zora Neale Hurston wrote with style and verve where love is concerned. To the reader, there is little doubt that the author believes love is the single most important thing in life. But what was Hurston's own experience?

First Love

In her younger years, Zora was a tomboy. Not only did she play with the Eatonville boys; she also roughhoused with them. Later she admitted having been something of a bully. And that is how she approached relations with the opposite sex during her early years—as confrontation, rather than intimacy.

Very likely, we will never know just what happened to Zora during the "lost" years, those which she described as having lived in a "shotgun" house. Was there a marriage? Not according to the legal records. Was there

Love and Its Discontents   65

While Hurston had a series of love affairs and three marriages, she channeled most of her energy into her work.

a relationship, tinged with physical abuse? That is our best guess.

Zora experienced crushes during her teenage years, but they all seem to have evaporated in a short time. Far different was her first real love, a man she met while at Howard University:

> He could stomp a piano out of this world, sing a fair baritone and dance beautifully. He noticed me, too, and I was carried away. For the first time since my mother's death, there was someone who felt really close and warm to me…We got married immediately after I finished my work at Barnard College, which should have been the happiest day of my life.[1]

Even from the distance of a century, the reader can feel Hurston about to qualify her happiness: "But it was not the happiest day. I was assailed by doubts. For the first time since I met him, I asked myself if I really were in love, or if this had been a habit."[2] This was self-doubt projected onto the man she married. Hurston was capable of falling in love and remaining there for a long time, but she inevitably felt the walls closing in around her and scrambled to get out before it was too late.

The marriage lasted only a few short years. During much of that time, the couple did not live together. As her folklore research progressed, Hurston found herself happier and happier to be on her own.

The Great Flirtation

The place and time of their first meeting is uncertain. What is certain is that they took a powerful shine to each other. This has been said of many pairs, but it was especially true in the case of Zora Neale Hurston and Langston Hughes.

Born and raised in the Midwest, Hughes was quite different from Hurston in temperament. She was a spirited tomboy; he was a self-effacing man. What they shared was an abiding belief in the importance of the African American experience. Both wrote extensively. Both were impulsive, sometimes even compulsive, travelers.

In 1927, Zora Neale Hurston and Langston Hughes shared weeks together on the road. Did they become lovers? Even the most talented researchers have not been able to make a positive case for this, especially in light of Hughes's sexuality—some believe he was gay, while one biographer argues that he was asexual. It is quite possible that the two enjoyed each other's company in a nonsexual manner.

Both Hurston and Hughes were protégés of "Godmother" Mason—in fact, Hughes was responsible for introducing Hurston to "the Godmother." Fed up with Mason's controlling personality, he had the first falling-out with Godmother, while Hurston remained a faithful protégé for years. It was during this time that Hughes and Hurston fell out over ownership of the words of *Mule Bone*.

Mule Bone, the play at the heart of the conflict between Hurston and Langston Hughes, was not publicly staged until 1991.

Love and Its Discontents

Putting aside the question of intellectual ownership, one thing is for certain: both parties handled the conflict poorly. The separation was so clear, so unequivocal that the two seldom spoke again, even though they continued to be part of the Harlem Renaissance. Some have remarked that the fracturing of their relationship is one of the genuine tragedies of African American twentieth-century literature.

Mistaken Marriage

In June 1939, the same month that she recorded African American folklore for the Works Progress Administration, Hurston embarked on her second marriage, to Herbert Sheen. This marriage was even less successful than her first.

Within four months, the couple lived in separate quarters, and within a year they were wrangling in the courts. The marriage was a terrible mistake, and about the only thing Hurston could claim was that she had not told many people about it. The formal divorce came in 1943, at about the time Hurston returned to the East Coast from California.

But she did not learn the full import of her mistake: Like her *Their Eyes Were Watching God* protagonist, Janie Crawford, Hurston married one more time. On this occasion, she kept it almost a complete secret. This turned out to be wise because the marriage ended almost as quickly as it began.

Labor over Love

Having given up on marriage, Hurston had a short run of flirtations. The best known was with British-born Fred Irvine. The owner of a powerboat, and a Renaissance man interested in all manner of things, Irvine planned to go to the Caribbean with Hurston. The trip never took place, but their friendship lasted for years, and it was likely a great source of happiness for Hurston.

Hurston seldom, if ever, expressed self-pity. She was too aware of the terrible things that can and often do happen in the world. But she did strike an intriguing note in her discussion of love in her autobiography:

> Perhaps the oath of Hercules shall always defeat me in love. Once when I was small and first coming upon the story of the Choice of Hercules, I was so impressed that I swore an oath to leave all pleasure and take the hard road of labor. Perhaps God heard me and wrote down my words in His book.[3]

While she may not have found an enduring marriage or romantic relationship, she undoubtedly channeled all of her spirit, intellect, and love into her work.

Chapter 9

Adversity

Anyone who studies Zora Neale Hurston's life marvels at the difficulties she faced up to the age of fifty. But those who go beyond find that her hardships did not lessen. If anything, problems only piled up as the years wore on. Through it all, she retained a sharp, steady sense of self.

The Advent of World War II

Hurston had never been overly interested in politics. But the last years of the Great Depression pulled something out of her, something she had long denied. There was bitterness behind her often cheerful, laughing expression.

Sometime prior to December 7, 1941—the date of the Japanese attack on Pearl Harbor—Hurston penned an essay entitled "Seeing the World as It Is," initially intending it for her autobiography, *Dust Tracks on a Road*. At the request of her publishers, the chapter was removed from the final book. It's easy to understand why

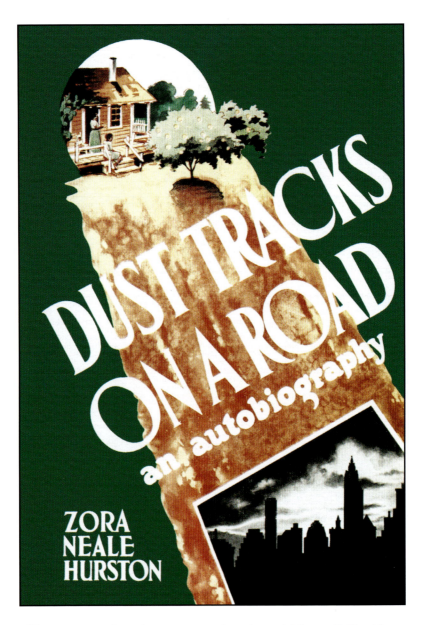

Hurston was forced to remove lengthy criticism of President Franklin Roosevelt from her autobiography, *Dust Tracks on a Road*, published at the height of World War II in 1942.

the publisher was uneasy; for the time, Hurston's views were controversial and nearly heretical:

> All around me, bitter tears are being shed over the fate of Holland, Belgium, France, and England. I must confess to being a little dry around the eyes. I hear people shaking with shudders at the thought of Germany collecting taxes in Holland. I have not heard a word against Holland collecting one twelfth of poor people's wages in Asia. Hitler's crime is that he is actually doing a thing like that to his own kind.[1]

While Hurston was obviously not an admirer of Hitler, her ideas about Western imperialism had crystallized, however, and she felt strongly that the United States and its allies were not unambiguously "good guys" either. Everywhere she saw evidence of the negative hand of the Western nations. She then went even further in her criticism of President Franklin Roosevelt:

> President Roosevelt could extend his four freedoms to some people right here in America before he takes it all abroad, and no doubt, he would do it too, if it would bring in the same amount of glory…He can call names across an ocean, but he evidently has not the courage to speak even softly at home…I wish that I could say differently, but I cannot. I will fight for my country, but I will not lie for her.[2]

While this was an accurate and clear-eyed view of America's problem of racial inequality, words like these were risky even before America entered World War II.

Once the nation geared up for that enormous contest, they became downright dangerous.

Escape to the West

Hurston spent a year or two in sunny southern California, writing scripts for what might have become screenplays. She never experienced much success on the West Coast, but, like many East Coast Americans, she found aspects of California life marvelous, especially the bright sunshine. By the end of the Second World War, she was back on the East Coast, dividing her time between Harlem and Florida. But peace—and rest—were about to be denied her.

Roads Not Taken

Zora Neale Hurston seldom expressed sadness or regret. She regarded life as a grand adventure, and she believed it necessary to weather the trying moments. But there were times when she cast a sigh of regret for having divorced Herbert Sheen. While Hurston struggled with finances and occasional poor health, Sheen went on to become a successful physician in California. They kept in touch by letter, almost to the time of Hurston's death.

Adversity 75

In a bitter twist, the *New York Age*, a publication founded by Hurston supporter Timothy T. Fortune (*pictured*), would go on to print unfounded and ultimately false accusations against Hurston.

False Charges

In 1948, while living and working in Harlem, Hurston was suddenly accused of sexual molestation of a minor. Though they came out of left field, the charges were devastating to a person who prided herself on proper behavior, even while she lived an eccentric lifestyle.

The specifics were as follows: one ten-year-old boy, the son of a former landlady, made the accusation and was supported by three others. They accused Hurston—along with other adults whom Hurston had never met—of performing sexual acts with the boy almost every afternoon in the same basement of the apartment house.

The charges themselves were nasty and later found to be false—the entire matter could have stayed private, as it was confined to juvenile court, where the proceedings would be kept confidential and the records sealed. But a court employee leaked the story to two prominent black publications, the *New York Age* and the *Afro-American*, which reprinted the charges and accusations without waiting for evidence to emerge. For Hurston, this was a deep betrayal by her own community, and an especially cruel irony as Hurston was once mentored by the founder of the *New York Age*, Timothy T. Fortune. She was utterly devastated. Had she been left to her own devices, she might well have committed suicide. Instead, she was rescued by a small group of loyal friends.

Carl Van Vechten (whom Hurston addressed as "Carlo") was her staunchest ally. Fannie Hurst was a close second. They came to Hurston's rescue with friendship, solace, and financial support. Even so, it was a traumatic event that very nearly ruined her life. While Hurston did beat the charge and was acquitted, she was scarred for life. She was heartsick and desperately angry at the black community, which she felt abandoned by.

"I care nothing for anything anymore," Hurston wrote to a pair of friends. "My country has failed me utterly. My race has seen fit to destroy me without reason, and with the vilest tools conceived of by man so far."[3] Later, she went so far as to write that if someone were to design a new republic, or nation, of African Americans, she would be the first to depart the area because she could not bear the thought of being governed by so ungrateful a people. Clearly, the wound had been deep.

Return to Florida

Still injured from the false charges and her subsequent bad press, Hurston felt ready to leave Harlem. By early 1950, she had settled in Florida for good. She had tried the North—New York City especially—for decades and found that the Sunshine State was the best for her health, mental and physical. In letters to her Harlem friends, Hurston was cheery and upbeat, saying her troubles were at last behind her. In truth, she was very low on funds, and her spirits were not much better. One thing she did not anticipate was being found out as a housemaid.

Down on her luck, Hurston had few options, ultimately choosing to work as a maid in a well-to-do white home. The local newspaper reported that she had been "found out" as a writer by her employer, who happened to see an essay that Hurston had written for the

The landmark ruling in *Brown v. Board of Education* overturned the practice of segregation in American schools.

Adversity

Saturday Evening Post. In the newspaper article, Hurston claimed that years of mental work had led her to resume work with her hands and that it was entirely by her own choice. Most readers saw through the disguise, however, and Hurston received a warm wash of pity, which she absolutely despised.

As she grew older, Hurston became less able to restrain her responses. She loathed the notion of pity, whether it came from white or black people. And she increasingly set herself at odds with the move toward racial desegregation. Perhaps the most influential—and damaging—thing she ever wrote was printed in 1955.

A Controversial Opinion

In May 1954, the US Supreme Court handed down its single most important decision regarding race relations with *Brown v. Board of Education.* The notion of "separate but equal" was inherently unequal, the Court declared, and the nation's public schools must move toward integration of the races. The Court's ruling drove an even stronger wedge into the racial divide. Many people—white and black—hailed the ruling, while many others—including some black citizens—spoke out strongly against it. Hurston's statement on the issue surprised many, perhaps most, of her followers and fans, who decided she was hopelessly behind the times.

Writing in the *Orlando Sentinel*, Hurston described her opposition to the Supreme Court ruling in *Brown v. Board of Education*. Blacks and whites were inherently equal, she declared, and there was no reason, or need, for the high court to declare it so. "The whole matter revolves around the self-respect of my people," Hurston wrote. "How much satisfaction can I get from a court order for somebody to associate with me who does not wish me near them?...I regard the ruling of the U.S. Supreme Court as insulting...I see no tragedy in being too dark to be invited to a white social affair."

For a person who had grown up in all-black Eatonville, this statement was close to the whole truth. Hurston came to maturity in a town where black men and women managed and governed themselves, and were proud to do so. But the success of Eatonville had not been replicated in enough other towns and regions. Millions of African Americans in 1955 wished to achieve racial integration, and Hurston simply was not in step with their wishes.

Chapter 10

Rebirth

As her life approached its end, Zora Neale Hurston seemed right back where she started. She spent her last years primarily in Florida, among relatively poor communities of African Americans. Some of the people she encountered knew of her accomplishments, but many others did not. Hurston showed great confidence and personal security in what she had done over the course of her career. If people knew of Hurston's writing, then that was fine. If they did not? Just as fine.

The Last Years

Hurston was in Fort Pierce, Florida, by 1956. Though she did not realize it, this would be the last of many moves. Just 20 miles (32 km) from Miami, Fort Pierce was a largely African American town, with many kinds of people Hurston recognized from her past. They were the same sturdy, self-reliant people she had known in

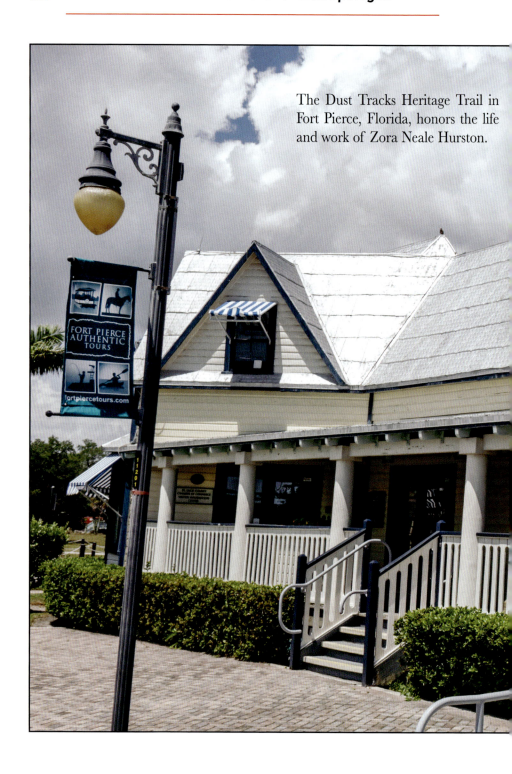

The Dust Tracks Heritage Trail in Fort Pierce, Florida, honors the life and work of Zora Neale Hurston.

Rebirth 83

Eatonville, although they had a broader knowledge of the world. She became a minor celebrity among these people. Local teenagers often came to her house to offer help, while middle-aged and older black residents came by to hear her many stories. Long afternoons filled with picnics and storytelling formed the happiest part of Hurston's final years.

But financial difficulties haunted her. She worked for a brief time as a librarian and then as a substitute teacher at a local school. In both jobs, she was undervalued and underpaid. She was fired from both. Plenty of bitterness could have resulted, but that sentiment does not seem to have been uppermost in her mind. Rather, Hurston appreciated how far she had come. Though she was in poor health and difficult financial circumstances, she never went hungry. And there were loads of memories of her incredible past.

One great project remained. Hurston spent much of the last five years of her life working on a biography of Herod the Great, the king who ordered the wholesale massacre of infants in biblical times.

What led Hurst to study the life of Herod the Great, one wonders? She had always been interested in the Bible as literature and showed this most effectively in *Moses, Man of the Mountain*. But during the last years of her life, she was keenly interested in Herod as a historical and biographical subject, rather than a literary one. She believed he had been mistreated by historians, and his complex story could shed light on the times in which she lived.

Thoroughly entranced by her subject, Hurston came to see Herod as a maligned figure whose life would serve as an important tale for contemporary times. One of her last surviving letters was sent to Harper Brothers Publishers:

Dear Sirs:

This is to query you if you would have any interest in the book I am laboring upon at present—a life of Herod the Great. One reason I approach you is because you will realize that any publisher who offers a life of Herod as it really was, and naturally different from the groundless legends which have been built up around his name has to have courage.

Sincerely Yours,

Zora Neale Hurston[1]

The downward slant of Zora's handwriting suggests the waning of both her physical and mental powers. Her book about Herod would never come to pass: She suffered two strokes and died after a brief hospitalization in January 1960.

Lost Again

While some of the early years of Hurston's life, primarily between 1912 and 1917, were virtually "lost," she was "lost" again in the decade that followed her death.

Major events in African American life and the destiny of the nation occurred in the 1960s, perhaps the most turbulent decade the United States had ever seen. Hurston was almost completely forgotten, and those that

86 ZORA NEALE HURSTON: Author and Anthropologist

Author Alice Walker championed Hurston's work, which had largely fallen into obscurity.

discussed her earlier writing did so from the point of view that her work was "quaint," an example of a failed style. But this changed in the 1970s, when a new young African American novelist went "looking for Zora."

Alice Walker's Pilgrimage

Born in rural Georgia in 1944, Alice Walker grew up in ways that mirrored Zora Neale Hurston's experience. The fifty-three years separating the two allowed Walker to become a successful novelist, focusing on feminist and African American themes. As her thirtieth birthday approached, Walker went in search of Hurston. She went first to Eatonville, but discovered that Hurston spent her last years in Fort Pierce.

Traveling farther south, Alice Walker spoke with people who had known Hurston in her last years. Primary among them was an African American physician who had rented a house to Hurston and spent much time in her company. From Clem Benton, Alice Walker learned that Hurston was destitute and in poor health, but her strong spirit endured. "She couldn't really write much near the end," Benton declared. "She had the stroke and it left her weak; her mind was affected. She couldn't think about anything for long." But these sad words were more than balanced by his memory of her earlier vitality. "She was always studying. Her mind—before the stroke—just worked all the time."[2] And perhaps most important, Benton recalled the outpouring of love at her funeral.

Hurston was laid to rest in the local African American cemetery, but there was no headstone until Alice Walker

ZORA NEALE HURSTON: Author and Anthropologist

Though it did not receive the recognition it deserved when Zora Neale Hurston was alive, Hurston's work has been rediscovered and rightly celebrated for its deep insight and value.

Rebirth 89

commissioned one. The visitor to that cemetery today finds the stone with these words:

> ZORA NEALE HURSTON
> "A Genius of the South"
> Novelist Folklorist
> Anthropologist
> 1901 to 1960[3]

In the place she was laid to rest, Hurston had the last laugh: she is still counted as being ten years younger than her actual age.

From Lost to Found

Alice Walker's pilgrimage had a powerful, even decisive effect: Zora Neale Hurston became known once more, still speaking to readers of our time. Millions of people, many of them high school and college students, have read *Their Eyes Were Watching God.* Hurston's other novels and stories receive some attention as well, but *Their Eyes Were Watching God* remains her claim to immortality.

No record of Hurston's last words survives. But a passage in her autobiography points in the direction she sought: "I do not pretend to read God's mind…I do not choose to admit weakness…Life, as it is, does not frighten me since I have made my peace with the universe as I find it, and bow to its laws."[4]

Though she may have slipped into obscurity for a time, Zora Neale Hurston has not been forgotten. For a girl from Eatonville to participate in the Harlem Renaissance, for a bright young woman to become a Barnard graduate, and for a lost writer to be found—all of these are triumphs and well worth remembering.

Chronology

1891
Zora Neale Hurston is born in rural Alabama.

1893
The Hurston family moves to Eatonville, Florida.

1905
Lucy Potts Hurston dies, and the family is scattered.

1911-1915
Zora experiences her "lost years."

1917
Zora enters Morgan Academy in Baltimore.

1922
Hurston earns an associate of arts degree from Howard University.

1925
She arrives in New York City.
She wins second place in the *Opportunity* contest for "Spunk."
The Harlem Renaissance is formally kicked off by publication of *The New Negro*.

1927
Hurston goes to Florida to collect African American folklore. Introduced to Charlotte Osgood Mason, Hurston soon becomes a protégé.

1928
Hurston interviews Cudjo Lewis.

1929
The Great Depression begins with the stock market crash in October.

1931
Hurston breaks with Langston Hughes over ownership of a play.

1934
Jonah's Gourd Vine is published by J. B. Lippincott & Co.

1937
Their Eyes Were Watching God is published by Lippincott.

1939
Moses, Man of the Mountain is published by Lippincott.

1941
World War II begins with the Japanese attack on Pearl Harbor.

1942
Hurston spends a year in southern California.

1945
Hurston's bitingly satirical "Crazy for this Democracy" is published.

1948
Hurston arrested on a morals charge in New York City.

1949
Seraph is published by Lippincott.

1951
Hurston is found working as a housekeeper in Florida.

1955
Hurston writes an essay opposed to court-ordered desegregation.

1959
She suffers a first stroke.

1960
She dies in Fort Pierce, Florida.

1973
Novelist Alice Walker goes in search of Hurston's grave. Hurston is rediscovered as an African American novelist.

1990s
Her books start to be read in all major colleges and universities.

2018
Barracoon: The Story of the Last "Black Cargo," Hurston's work based on her interviews with Cudjo Lewis, is finally published.

Chapter Notes

Chapter 1
Railroad Ties and Long-Haired Ladies
1. Hurston, Zora Neale. Recordings, Manuscripts, Photographs, and Ephemera, at the Library of Congress, found online at www.loc.gov/folklife/guides/Hurston.html.
2. Ibid.
3. Ibid.
4. Ibid.
5. Ibid.
6. Hurston, Zora Neale. *Dust Tracks on a Road: An Autobiography*, edited by Robert Hemenway. Chicago: University of Illinois Press, 1984, p. 62.

Chapter 2
Triumph and Trauma
1. Hurston, Zora Neale. *Dust Tracks on a Road: An Autobiography*, edited by Robert Hemenway. Chicago: University of Illinois Press, 1984, pp. 18–19.
2. Hurston, pp. 20–21.
3. Hurston, p. 53.
4. Hurston, pp. 56–57.
5. Hurston, p. 84.

Chapter 3
On the Road
1. Hurston, Zora Neale. *Dust Tracks on a Road: An Autobiography*, edited by Robert Hemenway. Chicago: University of Illinois Press, 1984, p. 39.

Chapter 4
Back in School
1. Hurston, Zora Neale. *Dust Tracks on a Road: An Autobiography*, edited by Robert Hemenway. Chicago: University of Illinois Press, 1984, p. 142.
2. Hurston, Zora Neale. "Spunk," found online at historymatters.gmu.edu/d/5131.

Chapter 5
Godmother and Her Children
1. Hurston, Zora Neale. *Dust Tracks on a Road: An Autobiography*, edited by Robert Hemenway. Chicago: University of Illinois Press, 1984, p. 174.
2. Hurston, p. 175.
3. Hurston, pp. 175–176.

Chapter 6
Jonah's Vine
1. Hurston, Zora Neale. *Jonah's Gourd Vine*. New York: Perennial Library, 1990, p. 1.
2. Hurston, p. 71.
3. Hurston, pp. 151.

Chapter 7
Watching God
1. Boyd, Valerie. *Wrapped in Rainbows: The Life of Zora Neale Hurston*. New York: Scribner, 2003.
2. Hurston, Zora Neale. *Their Eyes Were Watching God*. Lippincott, 1937, repr. Harper Perennial, 1990, p. 2.
3. Hurston, p. 11.
4. Hurston, pp. 192–193.

Chapter 8
Love and Its Discontents

1. Hurston, Zora Neale. *Dust Tracks on a Road: An Autobiography*, edited by Robert Hemenway. Chicago: University of Illinois Press, 1984, p. 250.
2. Hurston, pp. 250–251.
3. Hurston, pp. 261–262.

Chapter 9
Adversity

1. Hurston, Zora Neale. "Seeing The World As It Is," in *Dust Tracks on a Road: An Autobiography*, p. 342.
2. Ibid.
3. Boyd, Valerie. *Wrapped in Rainbows: The Life of Zora Neale Hurston*. New York: Scribner, 2003, p. 397.

Chapter 10
Rebirth

1. Kaplan, Carla, ed. *Zora Neale Hurston: A Life in Letters*. New York: Doubleday, 2002, p. 771.
2. Walker, Alice. *In Search of Our Mothers' Gardens*. New York: Harcourt Brace, 1983, p. 112.
3. Walker, p. 107.
4. Hurston, Zora Neale. *Dust Tracks on a Road: An Autobiography*, edited by Robert Hemenway. Chicago: University of Illinois Press, 1984, p. 278.

Glossary

asexual A lack of desire to engage in sexual activity with another person.

augur Acting as a sign of things to come.

capricious Having shifting moods and feelings, being controlled by whims.

code switching A shift in speech patterns, use of slang, and affect engaged in by people of color as they switch from speaking in largely white-dominated society to people of their own racial and/or ethnic background.

evocative Painting a vivid picture.

exactitude Attention to detail and specifics.

fetishization An uncomfortable and usually predatory focus on a particular group of people.

heretical Going against accepted and/or sacred mainstream beliefs.

institutional racism Racial discrimination that becomes a part of society through habit and practice, not through law.

lifeway A set of cultural customs or practices.

patronage The practice of supporting artists by financing their projects and lives.

philanthropic Generous; trying to do good in the world, usually through financial contributions.

progressive Supporting or advocating ideas that encourage social reform, usually in favor of marginalized groups.

reticent Reluctant to speak with or share information.

Further Reading

BOOKS

Boyd, Valerie. *Wrapped in Rainbows: The Life of Zora Neale Hurston*. New York, NY: Scribner, 2003.

Hurston, Zora Neale. *Barracoon: The Story of the Last "Black Cargo."* New York, NY: HarperCollins, 2018.

Moylan, Virginia Lynn. *Zora Neale Hurston's Final Decade*. Gainesville, FL: University Press of Florida, 2011.

WEBSITES

Zora Neale Hurston
https://www.zoranealehurston.com/about
The official website for Zora Neale Hurston.

Zora Neale Hurston's Barracoon Excerpt
http://www.vulture.com/2018/04/zora-neale-hurston-barracoon-excerpt.html
An excerpt from *Barracoon*, Hurston's biography of Cudjo Lewis, finally published in 2018.

Zora Neale Hurston on Zombies
https://www.youtube.com/watch?v=YmKPjh5RX6c
An audio clip of Zora Neale Hurston explaining the Haitian belief in zombies.

Index

A
American Mercury, 47

B
Barnard College, 35, 42, 43, 54, 66, 90
Barracoon: The Story of the Last "Black Cargo, 47
Belgium, 73
"Bella Mina," 9
Benton, Clem, 87
Bible, 84
biography, 47, 67, 84
Boas, Franz "Papa," 35, 37–38, 43
Brown v. Board of Education, 79–80

C
Cake, Tea, 62
Civil War, 46
Clarke, Joe, 17, 33, 59
code switching, 54
Columbia University, 35
country stores, 17, 33, 59, 60
Crawford, Janie, 59–63, 70
"Crow Dance," 9, 11

D
"Dat Old Black Gal," 11
Depression, 51, 71
desegregation, 79–80
divorce, 69, 74
Dust Tracks on the Road, 70, 71, 89–90

E
Eatonville, Florida, 13, 14–21, 22, 28, 33, 39–42, 59, 64, 80, 84, 87, 90
Ellison, Ralph, 63
England, 73
"Ever Been Down," 11

F
Federal Writers' Project (FWP), 7
fellowships, 38, 56
fetishization, 46
folklore, 7, 12, 37, 38, 39, 42–43, 56, 69
Fortune, Timothy T., 76

G
Great Depression, 51, 71
Great Migration, 55

H
Haiti, 57, 59
Harlem Renaissance, 35, 69, 90
Harper Brothers Publishers, 85

Herod the Great, 84–85
Historic Sketches of the Old South, 46
Holland, 73
homosexuality, 67
Howard University, 33, 35, 66
Hughes, Langston, 49, 51, 67, 69
Hurst, Fannie, 76
Hurston, Bob, 27–28, 42
Hurston, John, 13, 15, 16, 22–23, 27, 42, 52
Hurston, Sarah, 27
Hurston, Zora Neale,
   as anthropologist, 7, 9, 11–12, 17, 37–38, 39–48, 56–59, 89
   in the Caribbean, 56–57, 59
   death of, 85, 87–89
   early years, 12, 13–18, 21–28, 64, 85
   education, 16, 30–38
   false charges against, 76–77
   later years, 77, 79–85
   legacy, 85, 87–90
   novels, 12, 51–55, 59–63, 70, 89
   personal life, 28–29, 64–70, 74
   as playwright, 28, 49, 51, 67, 69
   short stories, 33, 35, 51

I

imperialism, 73
institutional racism, 12
integration, 79–80
intellectual property, 51
Irvine, Fred, 70

J

Jamaica, 56–57
J. B. Lippincott, 52, 55
Jonah's Gourd Vine, 51–55
Journal of Negro History, 46
Julius Rosenwald Fund, 56
"jump at de sun," 15, 27

K

Kossula, 46, 47
Kossula: Last of the Takoi Slaves, 47

L

"Last Slave Ship, The," 47
"Let the Deal Go Down," 11–12
Lewis, Cudjo, 46, 47
Locke, Alain, 33, 49

M

Maroons, 56–57
Mason, Charlotte Osgood, 43–44, 46, 47, 48, 49, 51, 56, 67

Index

Morgan Academy, 32–33
Moses, Man of the Mountain, 84
Mule Bone, 49, 51, 67, 69

N

Native Americans, 9, 44
novels, 12, 51–55, 59–63, 70, 89

O

Opportunity, 33

P

Pearson, John, 52, 55
physical abuse, 28, 66
plagiarism, 46–47
plays, 28, 30, 49, 51
Poker!, 28
Potts, Lucy, 13–14, 15, 16, 18, 21, 22, 23, 27, 52
primitivism, 44
protagonists, 52, 55, 70
publishers, 52, 53, 55, 71, 73, 85

R

Rhodes Scholarship, 33
Roche, Emma Langdon, 46
Roosevelt, Franklin, 73

S

"Seeing the World as It Is," 71, 73
segregation, 16

"separate but equal," 79
Shakespeare, William, 30
Sheen, Herbert, 69, 74
short stories, 33, 35, 51
"Spunk," 33, 35
stock market crash, 51
strokes, 85, 87
superstitions, 17, 21
systemic oppression, 12

T

Their Eyes Were Watching God, 12, 59–63, 70, 89

U

US Supreme Court, 79, 80

V

Van Vechten, Carl, 76
voodoo, 17, 59

W

Walker, Alice, 63, 87–89
Watson, Phoeby, 60
working-class songs, 7, 9, 11
Works Progress Administration (WPA), 7, 69
World War II, 71, 73, 74
Wright, Richard, 63

Charlotte Etinde-Crompton

Samuel Willard Crompton

About the Authors

Charlotte Etinde-Crompton was born and raised in Zaire and came to Massachusetts at the age of twenty. Her artistic sensibility stems from her early exposure to the many talented artists of her family and tribe, which included master wood-carvers. Her interest in African American art has been an abiding passion since her arrival in the United States.

Samuel Willard Crompton is a tenth-generation New Englander who now lives in metropolitan Atlanta. For twenty-eight years, he was a professor of history at Holyoke Community College. His early interest in the arts comes from his wood-carver father and his oil-painter mother. Crompton is the author and editor of several books, including a number of nonfiction young adult titles with Enslow Publishing. This is his first collaboration with his wife.